DEDICATED TO MY THREE WONDERFUL BOYS...

©BRIAN GLENN INNERVISIONS 2017 ALL RIGHTS RESERVED

THE SCIENCE OF LIVING YOUR DREAMS

Brian Glenn

innervisions
school of clinical hypnosis

©BRIAN GLENN INNERVISIONS 2017 ALL RIGHTS RESERVED

CONTENTS

FORWARD..4

INTRODUCTION...5

THE HISTORY OF THE LAW OF ATTRACTION 8

THE BEGINNING OF TIME...10

ALBERT EINSTEIN 12

EXPERIMENT ONE 15

EXPERIMENT TWO 18

EXPERIMENT THREE 20

TELEVISION TRANSMISSIONS...23

THE HUMAN HEART 25

THE AMAZING LAW OF ATTRACTION 28

PROBLEMATIC QUESTIONS 31

THE RULES 39

FINALLY 47

INNERVISIONS SCHOOL OF CLINICAL HYPNOSIS 49

ACCREDITATION...51

DIPLOMA..53

FORWARD

During my lifetime, I have used this very energy source to inadvertently create sadness and misery in my life, and now as a result of research and wisdom, I understand it better.

I spent the past ten years learning, thinking and researching the Amazing Law of Attraction, and found the ability to harness this energy field and bring an abundance of anything I want into my life.

I am living the dream, and I would like you to live your dream too. With easy to understand science and real life stories and scientific research I would like to invite you to this amazing opportunity to introduce you to a new way of thinking.

A way of thinking that will inevitably change your life as you know it.

With love…

INTRODUCTION

Almost universally, ancient texts and spiritual traditions around the world suggest that everything in our world is connected in ways that we are only just beginning to understand.

They speak of an Energy field. This subtle field of energy is in fact described by western scientists as a net or a web that creates what they call the underlying fabric of all creation.

This field of energy has been here from the very beginning of time. It's an intelligent field, an intelligence that responds deeply to human emotion.

Modern day scientists call this invisible energy field 'THE ETHER'.

In 1944, Max Planck, The Father of Quantum Physics, shocked the world by saying that the Ether is where the birth of stars, the DNA of life, and everything between originates.

Recent discoveries reveal dramatic evidence that Max Planck's theory is real.

It's this missing link in our understanding that provides the container for the universe, the bridge between our imagination and our reality, and the mirror in our world for what we create in our beliefs.

It's the essence of a new scientific law that we are able to manipulate to bring all our hopes and dreams into reality.

To unleash the power of this energy field into our lives, we must understand how it works and speak the language that it recognises.

During my lifetime, I have used this very energy source to inadvertently create sadness and misery in my life, and now as a result of research and wisdom, I understand it better.

I spent the past ten years learning, thinking and researching the Amazing Law of Attraction, and found the ability to harness this energy field and bring an abundance of anything I want into my life.
I am living the dream, and I would like you to live your dream too.

With easy to understand science and real life stories and scientific research I would like to invite you to this amazing opportunity to introduce you to a new

©BRIAN GLENN INNERVISIONS 2017 ALL RIGHTS RESERVED

way of thinking. A way of thinking that will inevitably change your life as you know it.

To accompany this book, you are welcome to download my Movie of the same title, and a hypnosis audio track that will help you to manifest your dreams.

www.innerbook.co.uk/dreams.zip

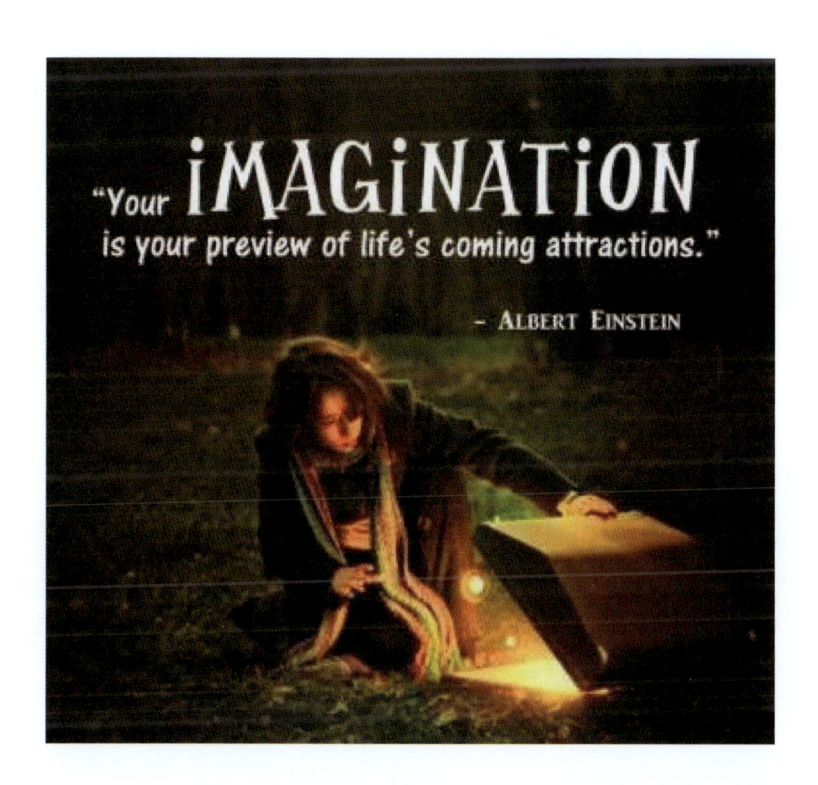

"Your IMAGINATION is your preview of life's coming attractions."

– Albert Einstein

THE HISTORY OF THE LAW OF ATTRACTION

Before we go too deep into the modern applications of the law of attraction, it is important that you understand that this is not simply New Age nonsense (most descriptions of the law of attraction refer to it as a product of a New Age Mentality). The principles of the law of attraction date back far beyond the new found popularity of the New Age.

Buddha was actually one of the first to introduce man to the law of attraction. He said, "What you have become is what you have thought." This was a principle that the people of the east were acquainted with for centuries before it began to sweep into the western hemisphere.

The concept of karma also may have drawn its roots from the law of attraction. Karma states that you will eventually be revisited by that which you have sent out into the universe. If you have practiced kindness and compassion, you will receive in kind. If you have been deliberately cruel to another, you will receive back into your life that cruelty which you have sent out.

Your actions and thoughts morph into physical entities, causing the universe to react in kind.

The law of attraction began to gain popularity in the western hemisphere in the 19th century, as people began to appreciate the power of positive thinking and apply it to their life.

This new concept was first introduced to the general public by William Walker Atkinson, the editor of New Thought magazine, who published a book called Thought Vibration or the Law of Attraction in the Thought World in 1906.

As you can see, the law of attraction is not new. The concept that thought can have a predominate effect on the course of a person's destiny has been taught by wise men throughout the ages, and has given rise to a whole new era of beliefs.

THE BEGINNING OF TIME

Let us start by going back to the beginning of time. Around the time 13 - 20 Billion years ago, the universe as we knew it then was around the size of a green pea, and about 1cm in diameter.

This was probably because all the things we consider to be space in between everything, for example the space between us and the planet, the space between you and I, and the space between myself and this computer monitor was all considered to be non-existent.

Everything was compacted down to the size of a green pea, and because of this, the energy that was created was something around 1 million million degrees Fahrenheit. We are not really sure it was exactly one million million degrees Fahrenheit, we just know it was very very hot.

Then one day something magical happened. The energy that was generated in this matter actually exploded (the big bang) and that created the universe as we know it today. It created what we consider to have space between everything now.

So now there is space in-between the planets, space between you and me, space between you and this computer screen. Space if you look at it in a kind of a scientific way was created.

The picture on the left is of the neural network within the brain. The picture on the right was taken by the Hubble telescope and is a picture of the Universe.

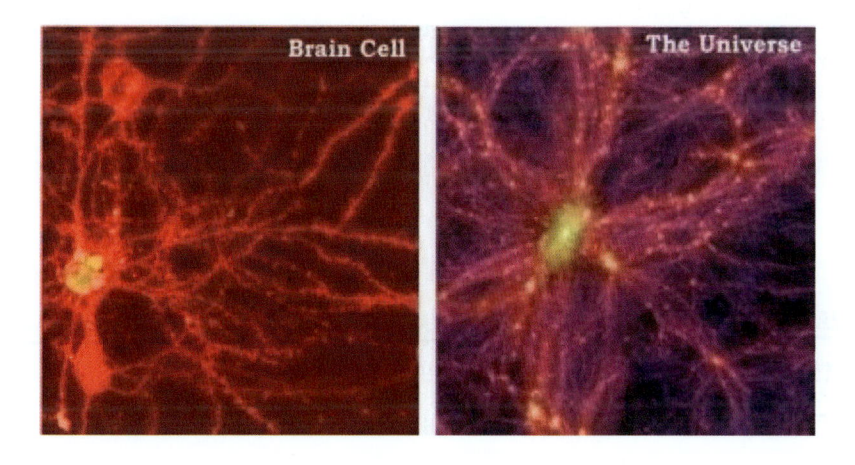

Brain Cell | The Universe

Notice the amazing similarities of the two pictures. This makes more sense of the passage seen in the bible "As above – So below"; indicating that the biggest things we see in the universe are similar to the tiniest things in the universe.

ALBERT EINSTEIN

Albert Einstein had a bit of a problem with all this space and stuff; he claimed there couldn't be any space between us, and nothing in that space, he considered there must be something in that space. It is not empty space, so he declared.

He proposed there must be something in there, and he referred to this space as the Ether. He considered that if there was nothing there, then there wouldn't be any ability to shine light through anything, because there is nothing to shine the light through. There would be no ability to hear things because there would be nothing to transmit speech through. So he considered there must be something in this empty space that he called the Ether.

Unfortunately he could not prove the Ether existed, nor did he have the time to explore this, so what he decided to do was task a couple of his colleagues to conduct a scientific experiment to see if the Ether really did exist.

In the year 1897 – Einstein tasked two of his colleagues by the name of Michelson and Morley to come up with a scientific study to prove or disprove his theory that the Ether existed.

Michelson and Morley went ahead and built up a model to prove or disprove whether the Ether existed or not. They concluded by this scientific study that the Ether did not exist. This of course confused Einstein even more, he didn't like that at all, Einstein was adamant that the Ether did exist.

Over the next century it was considered that the Michelson and Morley experiment was the most famous failed experiment of all time because they discovered one hundred years later that the Ether does actually exist.

In 1986 a gentleman by the name of E. W. Silvertooth, who worked for the United States Air Force, redid the experiment with more modern scientific equipment and he actually proved that the Ether does exist.

The Ether goes by lots of different names as it doesn't have an official name yet because it's still so young. Some people call it

- The Quantum Hologram
- The Field
- The Mind Of God
- Natures Mind
- The Matrix

In more recent times there have been lots of experiments conducted to look at what is actually happening in this energy field. What I would like to do now is share three experiments that are very interesting and look at the energy field that we are talking about and how we can use that energy field to attract things into our lives.

EXPERIMENT ONE

This experiment took place in Geneva on 25th July 1997 in the particle accelerator that exists there. Imagine an underground tunnel that goes seven miles in one direction and seven miles in the other direction. What they did in Geneva was place a photon right in the middle as show in the diagram below.

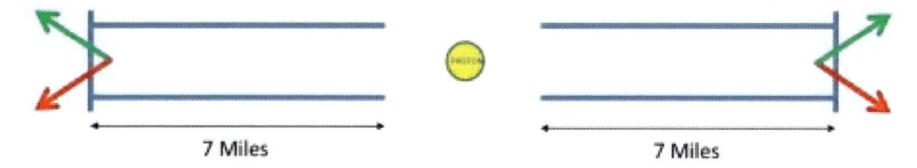

7 Miles   7 Miles

A photon of course is what everything is made up from. The photon was placed in the middle and then split into two and then the experiment began.

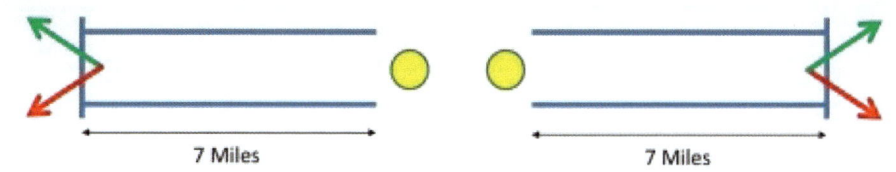

7 Miles   7 Miles

They fired each photon in the opposite directions all the way down to the end of the tube.

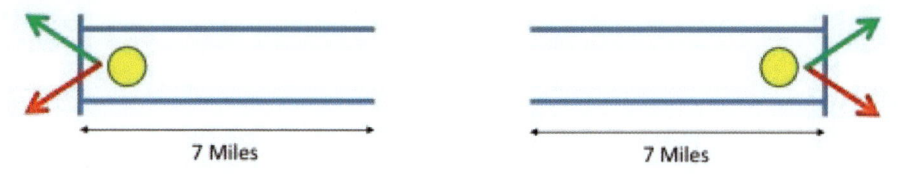

7 Miles   7 Miles

This in itself is not that difficult and not that unique, but what they found was when they took one of the photons, for example the one on the left and sent it up the green pathway, the right hand one also took the green pathway. And if they took the right hand one and sent it down the red pathway, the left one also went down the red pathway.

7 Miles   7 Miles

They considered this to be caused by the fact that the two photons were communicating with each other.

On further study they considered that the two photons could be communicating with each other, and if this was the case then there must be a time lapse between the communication. When looking at how long this time lapse was they realised there wasn't any and that it happened instantaneously.

For example if they sent the left hand photon up the green path, the right hand photon immediately went up the green path with no time lag, which proves without any doubt whatsoever that both photons are still connected together; a bit like when you see birds fly in the sky, when one turns, they all turn together, and with a shoal of fish when one turns, they all turn.

This experiment concluded that we are still connected. After all, as human beings we are also made of photons; so this proves we are all still connected, despite the big bang theory.

This theory was given a unique name. QUANTUM ENTANGLEMENT.

EXPERIMENT TWO

This experiment was conducted in 1992 by a Russian Scientist Vladimir Poponin. This scientist is famous for discovering what is now known as

'The Phantom DNA Effect'.

He created a vacuum inside a tube. The only thing left inside that tube after creating the vacuum was randomly placed photons; photons being present everywhere.

He then took a piece of human DNA and he put this human DNA inside this vacuum that had nothing in it but photons. When he put human DNA inside something amazing happened.

All the photons inside that vacuum took a linear form, they all lined up together; the photons were no longer random.

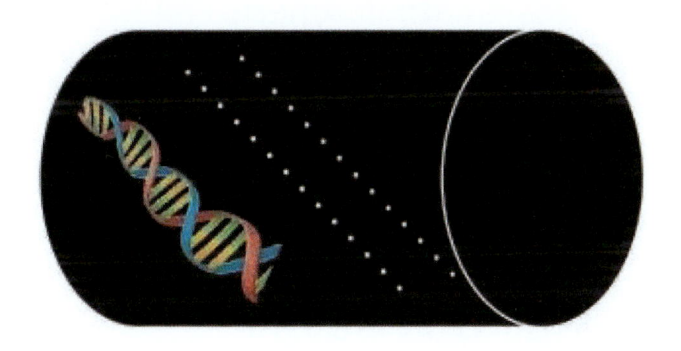

When he decided to remove the DNA from the vacuum something also amazing happened. He found that the photons that become linear remained linear they did not return to being random.

This experiment clearly suggests that human DNA has a direct effect on photons; just bear this in mind, because all these three experiments are now becoming very interesting.

EXPERIMENT THREE

This experiment was carried out in 1991 by the institute on Heartmath in America and it looks at the effects of human emotions on our DNA. The institute of Heartmath discovered that our emotions, whether negative or positive, have a direct effect on the properties of the DNA; therefore if we feel sad it screws our DNA up a little bit, and if we are happy our DNA has a more positive frame.

To do this experiment they took a piece of human DNA and placed the donor of the DNA in a different room. They then showed the donor various photographs and computer images of things that made them feel happy and sad, and they could see using scientific equipment a distinct difference in the human DNA, even though the human DNA had been extracted and no longer on the donor.

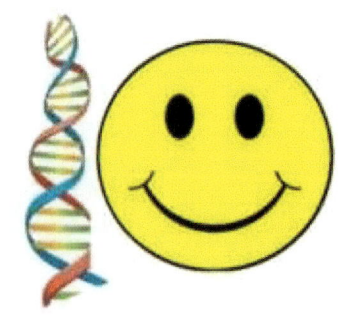

This experiment was later reproduced in a bigger sense in that the human DNA was taken to a completely different place in another part of the country, and the same effect happened. When the person's emotions changed so did the human DNA, even though they were miles apart. Once again this experiment does suggest that although the human DNA is no longer physically connected to the person, the effect is the same. It behaves as if it is still connected, although there is distance apart.

If we combine these three experiments together, what it suggests to us is that emotions change DNA and DNA changes matter. If we now cross out a few of those words we end up with a different thing altogether; it now suggests emotions change matter.

EMOTIONS ~~CHANGE DNA~~

~~DNA~~ **CHANGES MATTER**

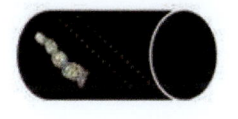

This is one of most important things regarding the Law of Attraction. It's all about your emotions. If you want to change the life that you live, you change and work on your emotions. Based on what we have learned so far let us now begin to take all this information into a slightly different frame where we can introduce the Amazing Law of Attraction, and make it work for you in a positive frame.

TELEVISION TRANSMISSIONS

Let us take a simplistic view of how TV signals work. This energy field we mentioned earlier, the Ether, has an amazing ability to carry radio frequencies, and this includes TV signals. Let us now have a look at how they work.

The image below is of the Emley Moor TV mast which transmits TV signals all around the Yorkshire area, and all around the region.

Depending on the strength of this transmission, we have the ability to collect it using a thing called a television set and all we need to do is tune in. We have the option to tune into hundreds of different channels these days but we only tune into the one we want. Ironically all the time you are watching one channel, the other channels are still there it's just that you haven't tuned into them yet.

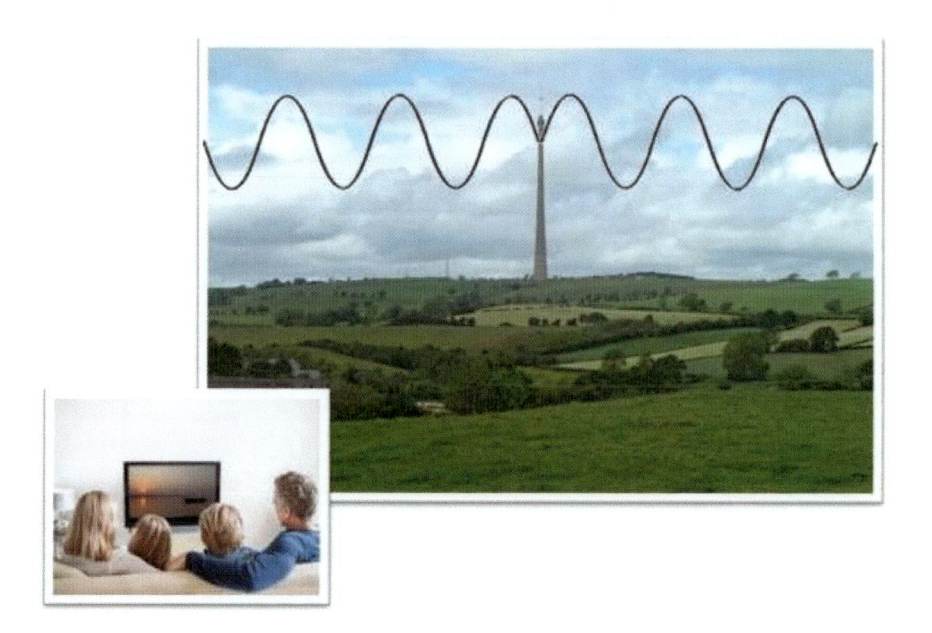

THE HUMAN HEART

The Institute of Heartmath in America have recently discovered an amazing thing about our heart. Let us take a look at some of the functions of the heart, some of which we already knew, and some aspects which are absolutely brand new, that you were not even probably aware of.

There are three very distinct functions that I would like to discuss with you, the first being quite simple, we already know that the heart is a pump, and it is designed to pump blood around our body to nourish all our organs and bring oxygen to them.

The second thing that you might not have been aware of is that it is a loving centre passed along through time through our ancient ancestors. They must have known that our heart was attached to emotions and love. I have never heard anyone say I love you with all of my kidneys, or I love you with all of my spleen, or I love you with all of my digestive system, it is always I love you with all of my heart. It is interesting that our ancient ancestors really did have all of this stuff sussed out. The third function of our heart which has been discovered in recent times, is that as the heart is beating, all it is really is a muscle that is contracting and retracting by receiving an electrical pulse which is generated within the human body.

Can you see where we are going with this? This electrical pulse is not dissimilar to the electrical signal that is put into the Ether from the TV transmitter. The only major difference being that your heart is obviously not transmitting TV signals into the Ether, your heart is transmitting your thoughts, feelings and emotions into the Ether.

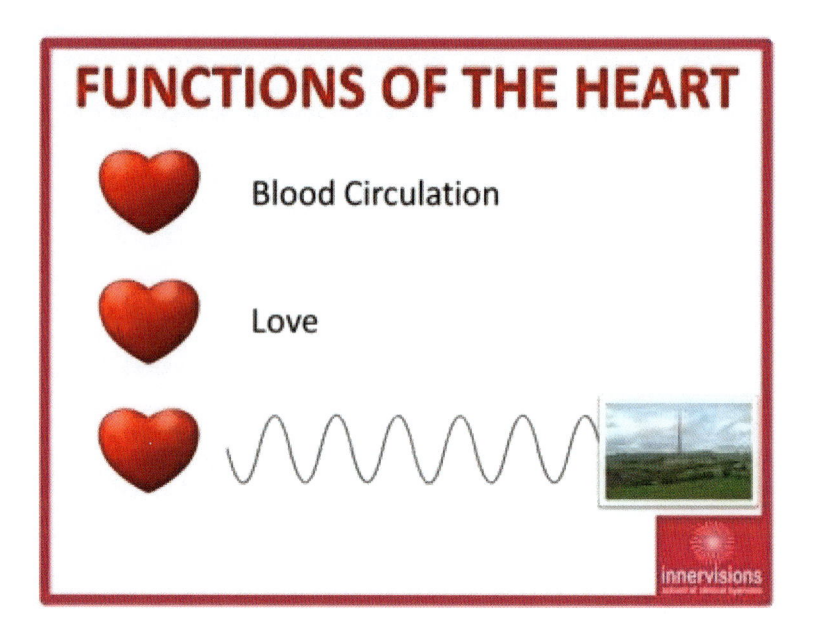

FUNCTIONS OF THE HEART

- Blood Circulation
- Love
- ∿∿∿∿∿

Consider this. What if those thoughts feelings and emotions that you are transmitting from your heart can be picked up by other people tuning into it just like your TV set does.

©BRIAN GLENN INNERVISIONS 2017 ALL RIGHTS RESERVED

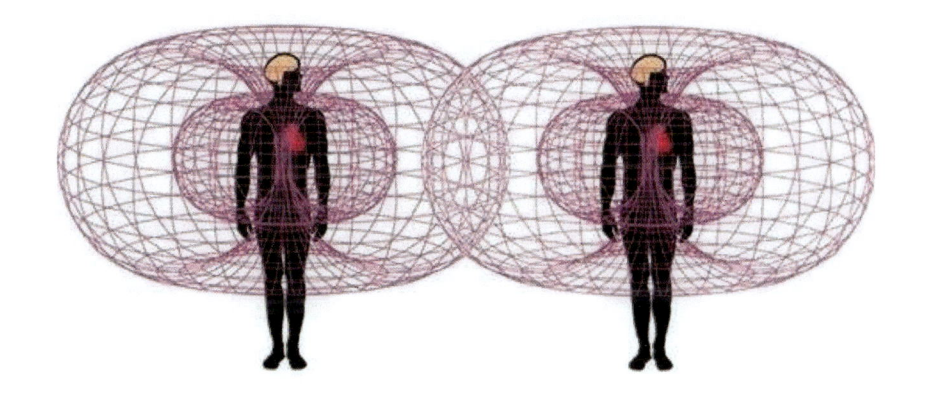

I wonder if this is where psychic abilities come from, where people can tune in to your thoughts, feelings and emotions from your past.

Also more importantly and even more interestingly, what happens to those thoughts, feelings and emotions?

They don't just disappear into the Ether... They find their way back to you, and this is what the Law of Attraction is all about. Your thoughts, feelings and emotions which you put out there into the energy field come back to you. Whether they are negative ones, or positive ones!

THE AMAZING LAW OF ATTRACTION

Whatever you think materialises as your experience.

Thoughts become things!

Here and now you are creating your own destiny, in accordance with what you allow yourself to think day by day. The things that enter your life are the expression of some belief in your own mind.

A metaphysician named Emmet Fox coined the term 'mental equivalent' to refer to this concept. For anything you desire in your life, whether that be a healthy body, financial prosperity or happy and fulfilling relationships, you must first supply a mental equivalent. This means you must form in your mind a clear and specific image of what you want as an end result. When you do this, it must come to you. And if there is anything in your life you don't want anymore, stop thinking about it. What we focus our attention on we get more of, so focussing on what we don't want just brings more of that into our lives.

The secret of successful living is to build up in your mind an idea of what you want. To do this, some people use the technique of visualisation, in which they mentally 'see' the new home, the world at peace, the completed book, the higher income, the new job or whatever it is they may want to bring about. Another technique is treasure mapping or creating a vision board. Constantly viewing the treasure map or vision board causes the mental equivalent to become firmly established in the mind, and then the person's outer experience eventually reflects it.

When you think about something you want and hold the image, it is attracted towards you. When you think about something you don't want and hold that image it is also attracted towards you. Whatever we think about we attract.

When we hear of someone else doing well or we see someone else having what we would like and we resent them or criticise them we are pushing away our own good. When we feel resentful we get more things in life to feel resentful about.

If we think life isn't fair then it isn't.

To get what we want we must focus on what we want, and only what we want. Protesting against war only creates more war; Mother Teresa always vowed never to attend an anti-war rally, or stop the fighting rally, but she regularly attended world peace rallies!

Railing against 'what is' only creates more of 'what is' while changing the focus of your thought onto what you want starts to create that instead.

You attract into your life whatever you think about. Your dominant thoughts will find a way to manifest; but the Law of Attraction gives rise to some tough questions that don't seem to have good answers. I would say, however, that these problems aren't caused by the Law of Attraction itself, but rather by the Law of Attraction as applied to objective reality.

PROBLEMATIC QUESTIONS

What happens when people put out conflicting intentions, like two people intending to get the same promotion, when only one position is available?

Do children, babies, and/or animals put out intentions? If a child is abused, does that mean the child intended it in some way? If I intend for my relationship to improve, but my spouse doesn't seem to care, what will happen?

These questions seem to weaken the plausibility of the Law of Attraction. Sometimes people answer them by going pretty far out. For example, it's been said by LOAers that a young child experiences abuse because s/he intended it, or earned it during a past life. Well, sure… we can explain just about anything, if we bring past lives into the equation, but in my own opinion, that's a cop-out. On the other hand, objective reality without the Law of Attraction doesn't provide satisfactory answers either — supposedly some kids are just born unlucky. That's a cop-out too.

I've never been satisfied by others' answers to these questions, and they're pretty important questions if the Law of Attraction is to be believed. Some books hint at the solution but never really nail it. That nail, however, can be found in the concept of subjective reality.

<u>Subjective reality</u> is a belief system in which (1) there is only one consciousness, (2) you are that singular consciousness, and (3) everything and everyone in your reality is a projection of your thoughts.

You may not see it yet, but subjective reality neatly answers all these tricky Law of Attraction questions. Let me explain...

In subjective reality there's only one consciousness, and it's yours. Consequently, there's only one source of intentions in your universe — YOU. While you may observe lots of walking, talking bodies in your reality, they all exist inside your consciousness. You know this is how your dreams work, but you haven't yet realized your waking reality is just another type of dream. It only seems solid because you believe (intend) it is.

Since none of the other characters you encounter are conscious in a way that's separate from you, nobody else can have intentions. The only intentions are yours. You're the only thinker in this universe.

It's important to correctly define the YOU in subjective reality. YOU are not your physical body. This is not the REAL you at all. I'm not suggesting you're a conscious body walking around in a world full of unconscious automatons. That would be a total misunderstanding of subjective reality. The correct viewpoint is that you're the single consciousness in which this entire reality takes place.

Imagine you're having a dream. In that dream what exactly are YOU? Are YOU the physical dream character you identify with? No, of course not, that's just your dream avatar. YOU are the dreamer. The entire dream occurs within your consciousness. All dream characters are projections of your dream thoughts, including your avatar. In fact, if you learn lucid dreaming, you can even switch avatars in your dream by possessing another character. In a lucid dream, you can do anything you believe you can.

Physical reality works the same way. This is a denser universe than what you experience in your sleeping dreams, so changes occur a bit more gradually here. But this reality still conforms to your thoughts just like a sleeping dream. YOU are the dreamer in which all of this is taking place.

The idea that other people have intentions is an illusion because other people are just projections. Of course, if you strongly believe other people have intentions, then that's the dream you'll create for yourself. However, ultimately it's still an illusion.

Here's how subjective reality answers these challenging Law of Attraction questions:

What happens when people put out conflicting intentions, like two people intending to get the same promotion when only one position is available?

Since you're the only intender, this is entirely an internal conflict — within YOU. You're holding the thought (the intention) for both people to want the same position. But you're also thinking (intending) that only one can get it. So you're intending competition. This whole situation is your creation. You believe in competition, so that's what you manifest. Maybe you have some beliefs (thoughts and intentions) about who will get the promotion, in which case your expectations will manifest. But you may have a higher order belief that life is random, unfair, uncertain, etc., so in that case you may manifest a surprise because that's what you're intending.

Being the only intender in your reality places a huge <u>responsibility</u> on your shoulders. You can give up control of your reality by thinking (intending) randomness and uncertainty, but you can never give up responsibility. You're the sole creator in this universe. If you think about war, poverty and disease etc., that's exactly what you'll manifest. If you think about peace, love and joy, you'll manifest that too. Your reality is exactly what you think it is. Whenever you think about anything, you summon its manifestation.

Do children, babies, and/or animals put out intentions?

No. Your own body doesn't even put out intentions — only your consciousness does. You're the only one who has intentions, so what takes precedence is what YOU intend for the children, babies, and animals in your reality. Every thought is an intention, so however you think about the other beings in your reality is what you'll eventually manifest for them. Keep in mind that beliefs are hierarchical, so if you have a high order belief that reality is random and unpredictable and out of your control, then that intention will trump other intentions of which you're less certain. It's your entire collection of thoughts that dictates how your reality manifests.

If a child is abused, does that mean the child intended it in some way?

No. It means YOU intended it. You intend child abuse to manifest simply by thinking about it. The more you think about child abuse (or any other subject), the more you'll see it expand in your reality. Whatever you think about expands, and not just in the narrow space of your avatar but in all of physical reality.

If I intend for my relationship to improve, but my spouse doesn't seem to care, what will happen?

This is another example of intending conflict. You're projecting one intention for your avatar and one for your spouse, so the actual unified intention is that of conflict. Hence the result you experience, subject to the influence of your higher order of beliefs, will be to experience conflict with your spouse. If your thoughts are conflicted, your reality is conflicted.

This is why assuming responsibility for your thoughts is so important. If you want to see peace in the world, then intend peace for EVERYTHING in your reality. If you want to see abundance in the world, then intend it for EVERYONE. If you want to enjoy loving relationships, then intend loving relationships for ALL. If you intend these only for your own avatar but not for others, then you're intending conflict, division, and separation; consequently, that's what you'll experience.

If you stop thinking about something entirely, does that mean it disappears? Yes, technically it does. But in practice it's next to impossible to un-create what you've already manifested. You'll continue creating the same problems just by noticing them. But when you assume 100% responsibility for everything you're experiencing in your reality right now — absolutely everything — then you assume the power to alter your reality by rechannelling your thoughts.

This entire reality is your creation. Feel good about that. Feel grateful for the richness of your world. Then begin creating the reality you truly want by making decisions and holding intentions. Think about what you desire, and withdraw your thoughts from what you don't want. The most natural, easiest way to do this is to pay attention to your emotions. Thinking about your desires feels good, and thinking about what you don't want makes you feel bad. When you notice yourself feeling bad, you've caught yourself thinking about something you don't want. Turn your focus back towards what you do want, and your emotional state will improve rapidly. As you do this repeatedly, you'll begin to see your physical reality shift too, first in subtle ways and then in bigger leaps.

I too am just a manifestation of your consciousness. I play the role you expect me to play. If you expect me to be a helpful guide, I will be. If you expect me to be profound and insightful, I will be. If you expect me to be confused or deluded, I will be. But of course there's no distinct 'ME' that is separate from 'YOU'. I'm just one of your many creations. I am what you intend me to be.

But deep down you already knew that, didn't you?

THE RULES

Following years of personal analysis, wondering why my life was so bad in my earlier years, I finally discovered the exact way that I was attracting negative events and situations into my own life.

I discovered seven rules that I was following precisely, and I wondered if I could use those same rules to bring a positive aspect to my life.

And today, I am living the dream by following those seven rules precisely, but now with a positive frame.

I would like to share these seven rules (and now an eighth one that I recently discovered) with you so that you and the clients you meet can also live their dream…

But the first step for you and your client is to take full and complete responsibility for who and what you are today.

Success through the law of attraction is to accept responsibility for the things that have occurred in your life, both good and bad. This is often the most difficult part of achieving success through manifestation, because we are taught from childhood to believe that our environment contributes in a large part to the circumstances in which we find ourselves. It's very hard to take the responsibility and acknowledge the fact that your environment was not the major contributing factor in each of these events; in many cases you will have no one to blame but yourself.

In order to help yourself move past these events, take a moment and write down on a piece of paper all of the major events in your life (again, both good and bad). Leave plenty of room underneath each one. Now, take a moment to go back and review these events. Write down what you were feeling at the time they happened, how you felt before they happened and what events had occurred prior to this. Chances are you are going to find that events occurring in your favour occurred at times when you were possessed of a positive attitude and other things in your life were going right. On the flip side, events which occurred probably happened concurrently with other events in your life which caused you to have a negative outlook on life. Coincidence?

Now let's take a look at the rules. Please be mindful that these rules need to be followed precisely – just like you always do in a negative frame. It's no good just following the one that you like or consider easy!

RULE 1: VISUALISE IT

It's very important to visualise (or focus on, or imagine) the END RESULT, and nothing but the END RESULT. Do not worry about the *how's* – you don't need to know how! – A good analogy to use is the sat nav in your car, you simply put the postcode in (end result) and the sat nav unit creates the journey based on the current road conditions etc. You just leave it to the sat nav to take you there.

Also, do not visualise it for more than 5 minutes a day. This is due to the law of reverse effect.

RULE TWO: FUEL IT WITH HEART BASED EMOTION

As we are carrying out rule one, we also incorporate this second rule at the same time.

Remember the law of dominant effect as part of your hypnotherapy training. Emotion is the key to most things. For example a simple informal prayer in a church will probably bring you nothing, but if you attach an emotion to the prayer, you are now using LOA to have your prayer answered.

So whatever it is that you choose in rule one, make sure you connect emotion to it. Imagine how it will feel when you have that end result. Get into that feeling emotion zone. It only needs to be for a few seconds!

The heart based emotion is similar to that feeling that comes upon you when you think about a loved one, a special friend, an animal or a new born baby. (In the negative frame, it could be fear, anger, shame, guilt etc.)

RULE THREE: BEHAVE LIKE YOU ALREADY HAVE IT

The thing you are asking for does already exist. It's just that you don't actually have it yet. So, during your daily activities and routines, behave like you already have it! – Instead of behaving like you don't. For example, naturally slim people don't bother going to Slimming World or counting calories do they?

RULE FOUR: TAKE ACTION

We humans have to actually do something physical to make this work! Just like you do in a negative frame! So you will need to do something physical and practical to manifest your dream!!

RULE FIVE: FOLLOW THE SIGNS

The universe is fantastic at showing you the absolute unquestionable right signs, but we humans are pretty crap at following them (unless it's in a negative frame).

Watch out for three signs or more; don't ignore them even if they take you out of your comfort zone. The universe must get fed up of manifesting stuff and trying to get you in a place to deliver it ;-)

RULE SIX: ACCEPT THE JOURNEY

This is probably the most difficult rule to understand and obey. When we are going through a bad time in our lives, we often see it as a negative and fall back into our old LOA thinking patterns and inadvertently invite more negative stuff into our lives. The reality is that the energy field we are tapping into (the universe) does not understand logic, or good and bad things, it simply manifests EXACTLY what you are asking for. So when you find yourself having a particularly painful and bad time, BELIEVE that the energy field has a divine plan based on what you asked for and is on with manifesting it.

Maybe the partner of your dreams happens to be the person in the car that ran you over and put you in hospital for a few weeks!!

RULE SEVEN: GRATITUDE

The energy field loves and adores gratitude. Stop focusing on the bad stuff right now, open your eyes and look around at the wonderful things you have in life. Animals, flowers, plants, a home, sons, daughters and children.

I have a friend who only has one leg due to an accident, and he thanks the universe every day for the one he has got!

Also, put a bit back into the energy field, do something for free without coming from ego. Every day plan and carry out some random act of kindness! Buy a stranger a lottery lucky dip ticket. Volunteer for something. Sponsor a worthy cause. Give someone a pound (or more).

RULE EIGHT: SURROUND YOURSELF WITH POSITIVE LOA PEOPLE!

I realised this eighth rule in more recent times.

As a human being, you will inevitably go through times that question your belief in all this stuff and you will soon resort to manifesting negative stuff into your life. For example, your partner may leave you and you start to focus on not having him/her! Or your focus on being alone. You then start to fuel it with negative emotion and before you know it, you are manifesting more of what you don't actually want.

Or a loved one becomes ill and you start to focus on their illness instead of their wellness. IT'S A TRAP!

During these times you will need your friends to teach you what you taught them!!! – And to keep you focussed on the right things. So start now to enrich your life by having a network of LOA'ers who will help you to maintain your ability to manifest wonderful dreams and not fall into the negative frame.

As a newcomer to this, you will need to deliberately take time daily to follow these rules. However, soon you will find that you start to use all the rules in a positive frame on auto pilot.

Personally, I never consciously follow these rules anymore; they have become a part of my life.

There are negative and positive examples of these eight rules on my video which you can download free here.

www.innerbook.co.uk/dreams.zip

FINALLY

Have patience; enjoy the journey to your dreams. Make adjustments along the way.

Don't do a test to see if it's real, this just shows that you have doubts and will prevent it from working anyway.

Don't think small, the universe does not know the difference between one pound and one million pounds. If you think small, small is exactly what you will get!

When you ask for stuff, be careful how you phrase it because it takes your words literally. For example it's no good saying 'I want to be slim', the universe will give you exactly that and you will always **WANT** to be slim. You must speak in the now, and as if you already have it. So 'I am now slim' would be a much better phrase to use.

Make a vision board with pictures of what you want accompanied by positive and carefully chosen phrases. Get the kids to make one with you too!

Have faith. Be mindful of what you are asking for during bad times, especially when you or loved ones are ill. Don't be telling your friends how poorly you or your friends are, the universe thinks you want more 'poorly'. Instead, either say nothing or tell friends how well they are, even if it's not true!!!

Be the change you want to see in the world. If you want world peace, be a peaceful person and stop falling out with your next door neighbour. If you want love on the planet, project love especially to people you don't particularly like or those who hurt you in the past. If you value life, stop killing things like flies, spiders, slugs, ants. They also have right to live!

It's all just matter of changing the way you think!

Thoughts become things – choose the good ones!

Bring it on!

INNERVISIONS SCHOOL OF CLINICAL HYPNOSIS

Established in 1996, Innervisions School of Clinical Hypnosis is the training provider of choice providing specialised training in modern clinical hypnosis. And with 21 years of training experience behind us, we are now one of the UK's leading training providers.

We aim to be the best in our particular field and to surpass our student's expectations; our teaching methods are unique, supportive, warm and friendly. We are dedicated to this profession and we intend to assist and train each and every student to become a competent practitioner in modern clinical hypnosis and hypnotherapy.

The course is designed to be of particular relevance to those in the caring profession as well as anyone who has an interest in the field of human potential and personal development. Whilst academic qualifications may be an advantage, we regard it as only being a small part of the learning curve to becoming a competent clinical hypnotherapist. This hypnotherapy training course is therefore open to those with a genuine interest in hypnotherapy irrespective of race, religion, and environmental classification, even though they may not have any relevant prior learning or training.

A UNIQUE OPPORTUNITY TO TRAIN FOR A REWARDING NEW CAREER

For two exciting days, Discover Hypnotherapy with our world class tutors and find out if hypnotherapy is the right career for you. You are invited to apply for a FREE place on our foundation weekend. Absolutely 100% free and unconditional.

www.innervisionsuk.com

ACCREDITATION

Our hypnotherapy training courses are fully supported and accredited by the General Hypnotherapy Standards Council.

Our practitioner level training course has been assessed and validated at practitioner level by The General Hypnotherapy Standards Council (UK). Graduates are eligible for professional registration with The General Hypnotherapy Register at full practitioner status.

GHSC
General Hypnotherapy Standards Council
Accredited Training

The GHSC was a key participant within the Working Group for Hypnotherapy Regulation whose primary purpose was to facilitate agreed standards within the profession and to subsequently bring about Voluntary Self-regulation (VSR), an officially recognised status, for the entire industry. To facilitate this, the Group actively co-operated with other industry representatives within the

Hypnotherapy Regulatory Forum (a body established by the now defunct Prince's Foundation for Integrated Health) and as a consequence VSR was finally established via the Natural Healthcare Council (CNHC) set up in 2008 with Department of Health funding - when it admitted Hypnotherapy into its regulatory system on 1st December 2010.

CNHC
Complementary & Natural Healthcare Council

DIPLOMA

Our Diploma in Hypnotherapy & Psychotherapy has been validated by the General Hypnotherapy Standards Council (GHSC) and Graduates from this course are eligible for professional registration with the General Hypnotherapy Register (the GHSC's registering agency) at full Practitioner status, together with the acquisition of the industry based award - the General Qualification in Hypnotherapy Practice (GQHP). .

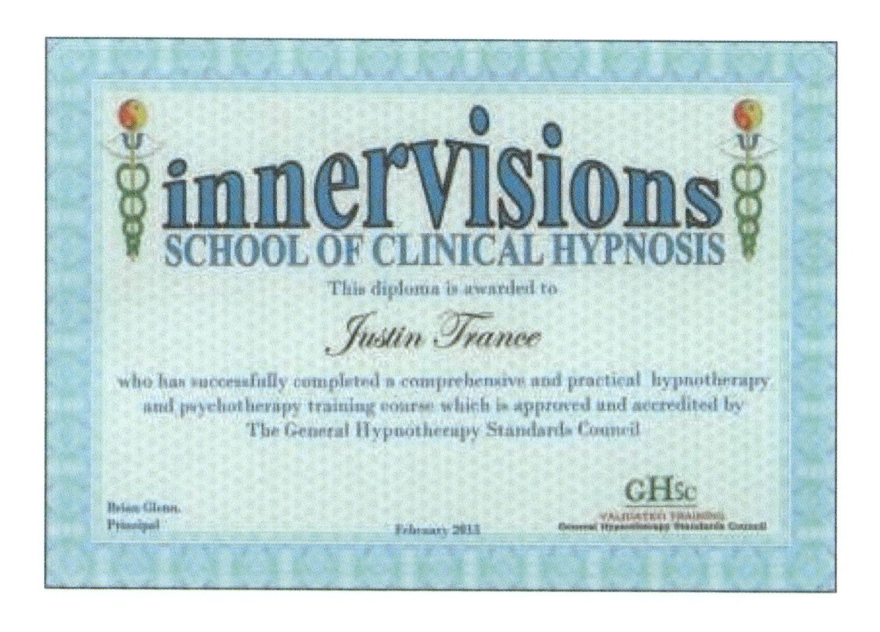

©BRIAN GLENN INNERVISIONS 2017 ALL RIGHTS RESERVED

Graduates of this course will also be eligible to register with the Complementary & Natural Healthcare Council (CNHC). For more information visit **www.cnhc.org.uk**

For two exciting days, Discover Hypnotherapy with our world class tutors and find out if hypnotherapy is the right career for you. You are invited to apply for a FREE place on our foundation weekend. Absolutely 100% free and unconditional.

www.**innervisionsuk**.com

Printed in Great Britain
by Amazon